City Life
Country Life

By Pamela Chanko

No part of this publication can be reproduced in whole or in part, or stored in a retrieval system, or transmitted in any form or by any means, electronic, mechanical, photocopying, recording, or otherwise, without written permission of the publisher. For permission, write to Scholastic Inc., 557 Broadway, New York, NY 10012.

ISBN: 978-1-338-88869-0

Editor: Liza Charlesworth
Art Director: Tannaz Fassihi; Designer: Tanya Chernyak
Photos ©: 5: Hongqi Zhang/Alamy Stock Photo; 7: Tetra Images/Alamy Stock Photo;
8: Tetra Images/Alamy Stock Photo. All other photos © Shutterstock.com.

Copyright © Scholastic Inc. All rights reserved. Published by Scholastic Inc.

1 2 3 4 5 6 7 8 9 10   68   31 30 29 28 27 26 25 24 23
Printed in Jiaxing, China. First printing, January 2023.

SCHOLASTIC INC.

What can you do in the city?
You can see tall buildings.
Let's go there!

What can you do in the country?
You can see big barns.
Let's go there!

What can you do in the city?
You can cross a busy street.
Let's go there!

What can you do in the country?
You can cross a quiet stream.
Let's go there!

What can you do in the city?
You can ride in a yellow taxi.
Let's go there!

What can you do in the country?
You can ride on a green tractor.
Let's go there!

city

country

What can you do in both places?
You can make a new friend.
Let's go there!